I0796279

DREAM JOBS If You Like TOYS

by Amie Jane Leavitt

CAPSTONE PRESS
a capstone imprint

Capstone Captivate is published by Capstone Press, an imprint of Capstone.
1710 Roe Crest Drive
North Mankato, Minnesota 56003
www.capstonepub.com

Library of Congress Cataloging-in-Publication Data is available on the Library of Congress website.
ISBN: 978-1-4966-8395-3 (library binding)
ISBN: 978-1-4966-8446-2 (eBook PDF)

Summary: Wouldn't it be cool to have a job working with or around the things you love? Are you passionate about toys? Perhaps designing new toys is an idea you could play around with! Readers will discover the possibilities of careers working with toys.

Image Credits
Alamy: Dinodia Photos, 28; Getty Images: picture alliance, 22; iStockphoto: Gregory Clifford, 24, syolacan, 29, Vesnaandjic, 10; Newscom: Laura Embry/ZUMA Press, 26, RICHARD B. LEVINE, 21, Wang Ying Xinhua News Agency, 20; Shutterstock: Blackshark66, 7, DAMRONG RATTANAPONG, 15, DeryaDraws, 13, DinosArt, 12, fizkes, 16, Gorodenkoff, back cover, 8, Magnia, (lines) Cover, MIKHAIL GRACHIKOV, (dots) Cover, Mikhail Rulkov, 4, Mikhail Zyablov, (toy) Cover, oneinchpunch, 18, ZikG, 17

Editorial Credits
Editor: Heather Williams; Designer: Sara Radka; Media Researcher: Morgan Walters; Production Specialist: Spencer Rosio

All internet sites appearing in back matter were available and accurate when this book was sent to press.

Printed in the United States
PA117

Table of Contents

Words in **bold** are in the glossary.

There are millions of jobs out there, but only a few are dream jobs. A dream job might not make you rich or famous, but you will be excited to go to work every day. If you love playing with, designing, or putting together toys, here are some dream jobs for you.

Toys can be for making music, counting, building, sorting, or just for having fun!

Toy Designer

Toys come in many shapes and sizes! They can be robots, trucks, or superheroes. They can be remote-controlled or stuffed. People buy toys from store shelves and websites. But who actually comes up with the ideas for all of these toys? Toy designers, that's who! Maybe someday that person could be you.

On the Job

Toy designers are kids at heart. They **brainstorm** ideas for toys. They draw them on paper or computer screens. Then they select their best ideas and build **prototypes**. These models help toy designers see if the toys they imagined will actually work. They often have to build many prototypes before they find the winner. There is a great deal of trial and error as designers try out different ideas.

FUN FACT

The oldest known toy in the world is a wooden doll. It was found in Siberia in Russia. The doll is 4,500 years old.

Pay Range

Average salary = $58,000 per year.

Education and Skills

Most toy designers have a college degree. Some do not. It is more important that toy designers have a good imagination. They need art skills and an ability to build different kinds of toys. They must also know how toys work. Toy designers also need writing and speaking skills to sell their ideas.

Playground Designer

What do slides, swings, monkey bars, climbing walls, and splash pads all have in common? They are all parts of children's playgrounds. These things are dreamed up by playground designers. Playground designers get to work with these toys all the time.

On the Job

Playground designers are artists. They are also scientists. They first look at the place where the playground will be built. Then they sketch out the different things they want in the playground, such as slides or climbing walls. They then look at these ideas from the eyes of a scientist. They decide if these ideas will be safe. For example, some structures might not be good to put in the hot sun. Designers also look at how the structures will fit in the space. They may need to adjust and make some parts smaller. They will have to make sure all of their ideas can be built with the money allowed too. Then they make a model. The model shows what the playground will look like when it is all done.

FUN FACT

Playgrounds aren't just for kids. Playgrounds are made for senior citizens too. Senior citizen playgrounds do not have monkey bars and jungle gyms. Instead they have outdoor rowing machines and stair steppers.

Pay Range

Average salary = $53,000 per year.

Education and Skills

Some playground designers get a college degree. They often learn how to create gardens or design buildings. Others are creative people who learn on the job. Playground designers have art skills. They like to make giant 3-D objects that encourage imagination and interaction. They also have math skills. They need to know how to fit certain-sized objects into a space. They also need to know how to budget money so they do not spend too much on the project.

Climbing walls are a fun addition to any outdoor playground.

Board games are a great way to spend time with friends and family.

Puzzle and Game Creator

Puzzle and game creators design crossword puzzles and word searches. They make jigsaw puzzles, card games, and board games. They even create electronic games. These creative people often work for large toy companies. Others work for newspapers and magazines. Some even start their own businesses. They make their own puzzles and games and sell them to people.

On the Job

Puzzle and game creators are always looking for interesting ideas. They might make a jigsaw puzzle out of a unique nature scene. Or they might make a card game based on numbers. Puzzle and game creators often work with other people. They get feedback from people who enjoy games and puzzles. If a puzzle or game is too hard or is not fun, the creator goes back to the drawing board.

FUN FACT

It took the inventor of the Rubik's Cube a month to figure out how to solve his own puzzle!

Pay Range

Depends on experience and type of puzzle or game. Board game creators make between $56,000 and $113,000 per year.

Education and Skills

College is helpful. But it is not required for most jobs in this field. Electronic or video game creators generally have a degree in computer science. People who make word puzzles have a good vocabulary. Those who create crosswords know many interesting facts. Game and puzzle creators are patient and willing to learn through trial and error. Most of all, puzzle makers have the ability to see possibilities in even the simplest of ideas.

An assembler puts most of the parts of a bike together before it is sold in a store.

Assembler

Some toys must be put together. Sometimes a machine does this. But often a person has to do it. That person is an assembler. Assemblers start with small plastic and metal parts. Then they use tools to put them together. The end result is a toy that kids can play with!

On the Job

Assemblers work in factories and in **retail** stores. They put together many types of toys. They put together small toys with special tools like tweezers. They also put together bigger toys like bikes and scooters. Workers on an **assembly line** might make the same toy every day. Or they might just assemble a certain part of a toy. Assemblers often work with other people to create their finished product.

FUN FACT

The Philadelphia Tin Toy Manufactory started mass-producing toys in 1838. It was one of the first toy factories in the United States.

Pay Range

Between $19,000 and $27,000 per year.

Education and Skills

Toy assemblers do not have to go to college. However, they should have certain skills. They need to know how to use hand tools and power tools. These include screwdrivers, wrenches, and drills. They must be able to see how small parts can be made into a whole. They must follow directions. It is very important to put toys together correctly. That way kids won't get hurt when they play with them.

Doll Clothing Fashion Designer

Dolls have many clothes to wear. They have swimsuits and coats. They have spacesuits and prom dresses. They have fun accessories such as purses and jewelry too. Doll fashion designers dream up ideas for all of these unique items.

Barbie dolls are the best-selling toy of all time.

On the Job

Doll fashion designers have a challenging job. How do they make clothes on a small scale? They first sketch their designs. Then they find materials to make the clothes and accessories. They use the dolls themselves as the models. They make sure the clothes are not too hard to put on and take off.

FUN FACT

The Barbie doll's full name is Barbara Millicent Roberts. It takes more than 100 people to make one Barbie doll with clothes and accessories.

Pay Range

Varies between $30,000 and $100,000 per year, depending upon experience and skills.

Education and Skills

Most doll fashion designers go to college. They learn about fashion or costume design. Others learn on their own. They use pen and paper to sketch designs. They also use computer programs.

Designing doll clothes is very similar to designing clothes for people.

Toy Inspector

A toy has been built. It is ready to ship to stores. But it can't be loaded onto the truck yet. First, it must pass through the hands of a toy inspector.

On the Job

Toy inspectors have a checklist for each toy. They use it to make sure the toy was built properly. They look over a toy to make sure all the pieces are in place. They examine the toy for possible safety issues. They run tests to make sure the toys work correctly. If the toys fail these checks, the toy inspectors write up reports. They also send the toys back through the line to be repaired. If a toy has a flaw after it is sold, it could be recalled. This means an item is pulled from the shelves and no longer sold. Companies do not want their toys to be recalled. This is why toy inspectors are so important.

Pay Range

Average salary = $38,000 per year.

Education and Skills

College is useful for toy inspectors. But it is not required. Most inspectors learn on the job. They need to look for details in things. They also need to be flexible. Their job can change every day. They will inspect many types of toys. Toy inspectors need to know how to use different kinds of tools.

FUN FACT

A toy called the CSI Fingerprint Examination Kit was recalled in 2007. Some people suspected it contained asbestos, a toxic powder that should never be handled by kids.

Broken or damaged toys cannot be sold.

Toy Reviewer

Most jobs in the toy industry are just for adults. But toy reviewers can be any age. Toy companies hire many kids to play with new toys. They want to make sure other kids will like the toys. Being a toy reviewer is a fun and exciting job for a kid.

On the Job

It isn't easy to become a toy reviewer. Many kids want this job. Toy companies send you free toys. Then you play with them and give the toy company your opinions. It's a pretty sweet gig!

The best toy critic is a kid who likes playing with toys!

Ryan's World released its own toy line in 2018.

Pay Range

Payment often comes in the form of free toys. Some companies do pay a small amount of money too.

Education and Skills

Toy companies hire kids from toddlers to preteens. Two requirements must be met to get the job. The kids must love to play with toys. They must also be able to tell what they think about the toys. If the kids are too young, their parents can help give the review.

FUN FACT

Some kids start their own review jobs online. Ryan of Ryan's World has done this. He has his own YouTube channel. Ryan tells kids what he thinks of toys. Many people watch his channel. He earns millions of dollars per year.

Pet Toy Designer

Toys aren't just for kids. They're also for pets. Many pets like to play with toys. Birds like to ring bells. Cats love pouncing on fake mice and jumping after feathers. Hamsters like to run in spinning wheels. Dogs like to chase balls and chew on squishy toys. Pet toy designers come up with the ideas for these toys.

Pet toy designers often test their designs with their own pets.

On the Job

Pet toy designers observe pets. They watch them play alone and with other animals. Then they design toys that are fun for the pets. Designers sketch out their ideas. Then they look for materials to make their toys. Some materials work well for some animals but not others. Some might create choking hazards for pets. Others might be toxic. This means the toy could poison the animal. A furry toy would also not work for an **aquatic** pet like a fish.

FUN FACT

More than 67 percent of U.S. households have some sort of pet.

Pay Range

Average salary = $55,000 per year.

Education and Skills

Pet toy designers can go to college. Or they can learn on their own. They should know a lot about pets. They can watch their own pets or the pets of others. This job is good for people who love animals and have a great imagination. It is also good for **entrepreneurs**.

New toys from companies all over the world are displayed at the North American International Toy Fair.

Toy Buyer

You may have noticed that some toys are sold at one store but not at another. Many retail stores hire toy buyers. These are people who decide what new toys a store will sell.

On the Job

Toy buyers travel often. They visit toy fairs around the world. This is where toy makers showcase their latest toys. Toy buyers move from **exhibit** to exhibit. They look at the toys on display. They play with them to see how they work. Then they decide which ones will sell best at their stores.

Pay Range

Varies, $50,000 to $66,000 per year.

Education and Skills

Toy buyers often go to college and study business. Most of them can tell what toys will be popular with kids and which ones will not. This is an important skill for this job. Retail stores do not want to buy toys that will not sell. This skill is more important than any college degree. Toy buyers must like to travel. They must also be comfortable talking with people. They talk to many toy makers at toy shows.

FUN FACT

The North American International Toy Fair is a well known toy fair. More than 30,000 toy professionals attend every year. The toy exhibits fill a space equal to seven football fields!

Toy buyers attend toy fairs to get ideas for new products and how to display them.

Children's Museum Employee

Kids get to play and discover at children's museums. They have fun at hands-on exhibits. They play with toys that help them learn new things. People who work at these museums must know how all of these toys work too. That way they can help the young visitors.

Children's museum employees create fun, colorful displays for guests to enjoy.

On the Job

Museum workers help set up the exhibits. They spend time playing with the toys so they know how they work. This lets them help children who visit. It also lets them fix exhibits that break down. There are many types of children's museums. Some are all about dinosaurs. Others teach about space and science. Some have mini train stations and fairy gardens too.

FUN FACT

The National Museum of Play is in Rochester, New York. It has a toy hall of fame, a coral reef, and a rainforest garden with real butterflies!

Pay Range

Average salary depends upon specific job and experience, between $31,000 and $54,000 per year.

Education and Skills

College is not required for basic jobs at a museum. However, directors and educators need a college degree. People who enjoy teaching and being one-on-one with children do best in this job. Museum workers must be experts on the items in the museum where they work. They also like playing with educational toys and being around people.

Game attendants yell, dance, and even sing to get people to come to their booths.

Game Attendant

You can play many types of games at a carnival or amusement park. At one booth, you can toss rings on a bottle. At other booths, you can shoot a ball into a hoop or throw darts to pop a balloon. The people who work these booths are called game attendants.

On the Job

Attendants must know how the games are played. They must also set up the games every time a new person comes to play. They award prizes to winners. Some attendants must also travel for their jobs. Carnivals often move from place to place. Amusement parks stay put. People who work at these parks don't have to travel.

FUN FACT

People who run games at carnivals are often called "carnival barkers." They "bark" to get people to play games and attend shows. "Come right up, don't be shy!"

Pay Range

Average salary = $24,000 per year.

Education and Skills

No formal schooling is needed. Most are trained on the job. Workers need to like games. They must also have a strong voice. Their job is to get people to come and play the games. They might yell out something like, "Come knock down these bottles and win a teddy bear!" They must also like to work in noisy, fast-paced places.

Retail Toy Salesperson

Many types of stores sell toys. There are big department stores. There are small toy stores. The people who work in these stores are called retail toy salespeople. They help kids find the toys of their dreams.

People who work in toy stores make sure the shelves are stocked with plenty of dolls, stuffed animals, games, and other toys.

On the Job

Retail toy salespeople greet customers. They ask what kinds of toys customers like. Then they make recommendations. These workers must know about all the toys in the store. That way they can tell customers about the toys. That means that part of their job is to play with the toys!

FUN FACT

Many people buy toys online now. Toy stores are coming up with ways to bring people back into the store. They offer fun events to their customers. They also give face-to-face service to customers.

Pay Range

Between $16,000 to $37,000 per year.

Education and Skills

College is not required. It is more important that people in this job like toys. They should also like to talk to new people and give them advice about toys. There is a lot of standing required at this type of job. Retail toy salespeople should also know how to run a cash register. They must know how to count money and give back change to customers too.

Puppeteers tell stories with their puppets.

Puppeteer

Puppeteers are people who work with puppets. They make toys come to life. They make the puppets move and talk. Puppeteers work at fairs, parties, and theaters. Some puppeteers work at amusement parks. Some work on movie sets.

On the Job

Many puppeteers make their own puppets. They use store-bought puppets too. Puppeteers create unique voices and personalities for them. They can work with one puppet or many puppets at a time. They can use a hand puppet or one attached to wires. Some use **ventriloquism** to make the puppet look like it is talking.

FUN FACT

Jim Henson came up with the term "muppet" in the 1950s. He came up with many muppets, including Kermit the Frog. Kermit wasn't originally green. The first Kermit was made out of Henson's mother's blue coat.

Pay Range

Average salary = $51,000 per year.

Education and Skills

Some puppeteers are trained actors. Others teach themselves. They might learn as an **apprentice** under a master puppeteer. Puppeteers are excellent storytellers. They love to entertain others. And they enjoy bringing toys to life.

Many puppeteers make their own puppets.

Glossary

apprentice (uh-PREN-tiss)—someone who learns a trade by working with a skilled person

aquatic (uh-KWAH-tik)—living or growing in water

assembly line (uh-SEM-blee LYN)—a group of workers and machines that puts together a product

brainstorm (BRAYN-storm)—to think of many ideas without judging them as good or bad

entrepreneur (ahn-trah-pri-NOOR)—a person who begins his or her own business

exhibit (ig-ZI-buht)—a display that shows something to the public

prototype (PROH-tuh-tipe)—the first version of an invention that tests an idea to see if it will work

retail (REE-tayl)—related to the sale of products or foods

ventriloquism (ven-TRILL-uh-kwiz-uhm)—when someone changes his or her voice to make it appear to come from somewhere else

Read More

Bebo. *The Everything Tabletop Games Book.* New York: Adams Media, 2019.

Benilan, Annabel. *Sewing Clothes for Barbie: 24 Stylish Outfits for Fashion Dolls.* Tunbridge Wells, Kent, UK: Search Press Limited, 2018.

White, Amy, Mark H. Pulham, and Dallin Blankenship. *Dressing the Naked Hand: The World's Greatest Guide to Making, Staging, and Performing with Puppets.* Sanger, CA: Familius, 2015.

Internet Sites

17 DIY Dog Toys You Can Make from Things in Your House
https://www.care.com/c/stories/6147/17-diy-dog-toys-how-to-make-fun-safe-toys-f/

How to Get Your Toy Made
https://makezine.com/2014/11/04/how-to-get-your-toy-made/

How to Sew Doll Clothes for Beginners
https://blog.treasurie.com/how-to-sew-doll-clothes-for-beginners/

Learn How to Puppeteer!
https://www.jimhensonsfamilyhub.com/home-1/2017/8/31/learn-how-to-puppeteer

Index